Author's Note: As with my first collection, *Tualco Tales.* the topics in this volume vary across a spectrum to include faith, fantasy, love, places, interactions and more. My hope again is that a discerning reader will find something of interest, value or maybe even inspiration among these pages.

This book is dedicated to Lisa, my wife, muse and travel partner.

Table of Contents

Away
Rules Are Meant To Be Broken
Ending
Repeat
Love My Life
You Again
Moments
Outta Here
No One
Musclehead
Lisa
Donnybrook
Blue Collar Blues
Ten and A Wakeup

Always

Your life should always be poetry and roses
candlelight dinners
nights under the stars
a sunset on the beach
your kids within reach
strong arms around you
to keep you warm

My arms are yours if you find them strong
enough
I'll give you all the love
there is in my heart
for you I could take
the world on my shoulders
keep my head high
with you by my side

And when our spring passes
summer fades
and fall's last leaves trickle down
I'll still be loving you
when my winter arrives
and my ashes are thrown
to the wind

Free

Brother I wonder
have you lost your way
or is it just my imagination

You always seemed to have everything
together
answers for everyone
pretty melodies
moving verse
now you're looking worse for wear

Brother is that fear in your eyes
or resignation
all those causes you fought for remain
years slip away
life grows shorter
there's no escaping the passage of time

Feel the spirit within you stir
the voice of the Lord
saying surrender to me

Call it conscience
call it what you will
you can't purchase grace
it's free
trust
and see it be

Encounter

Rising early
out of bed dressed
coffee brewed dogs tended to
traverse miles to reach the river
pull in park
dark gives way to morning

Cold December
dampening fog
out of the truck under dripping alder
maple Devil's Club spent blackberry vines
anticipation as the boots slip on
feel the adrenaline flow

No other vehicles
just one raving lunatic
muddy unkempt screaming into the trees
he glowers half snarls
as he walks past to the road
headed toward town and bridge

Watch warily
make sure he keeps moving
this isn't the way it used to be
worried about tweaking denizens
while pursuing a passion
out here alone and free

Shake off doubt
scramble through the trees
clamber down the bank to the river

rain left it high
barely fishable
just enough clarity to see

Slip into the water
past toppled tree snag
pull off line flip out a cast
clear plastic float swirls
inverted teardrop
chartreuse dot atop for visibility

At riffle's outer edge
bobber pauses, dips
rod tip strike sets the hook
prey yanks back twice
shakes, tugs
rips a line-stripping run for midstream

Silver rocket leaps full
splashes thrashes
flips subsurface somersaults
then bucking sulks deep
followed by two more leaps
and a grudging semi surrender

Coaxed to a break in the boulders
slowly not done yet
she surges twice more
feigns another run
finally eased into stiller water
onto a small bed of sand and gravel

Fish of a thousand casts

Oncorhynchus my-kiss
legendary Northwest steelhead
searun rainbow
nickel bright egg heavy
one less return to the hatchery

Success seldom comes as easily
much less repeatedly
another chilled hour time to head back
trudge past deep holes
downed limbs brush
through undergrowth limbs leaves

Partway upriver trail opens up
a campsite, blue tarps
barely smoking fire
try to slip by quietly
clearly no avail
haggard young woman stumbles from the tent

Stained jeans rumpled shirt
barefoot, scabs
wild matted dirty-blonde hair
she looks a little crazy
offers "Nice fish" hazily
smile missing a few teeth

Black lab out next
in a fog maybe inebriated
perhaps too tired to care
then a scream "I see you bitch"
pierces from upstream
resonating from the bridge through the trees

Momentary wonder
is there some way to help
no idea what that would be
"I see you" bellowed again
"I'm coming"
plenty of incentive to leave

Pick the way back
through brush
off the beaten path
reach the truck
lay fish in ice chest
head up the road for home

So many thoughts
conflicting emotions
what was my responsibility
live and let live
call or tell somebody
who what how much why

Any opportunity out
is a good day on the water
even in winter chill
yet can't shake the sadness
of drug induced madness
wonder what's happening to us

Lake Leo

Synapse crazy
lacy blue
bright moon, clouds oozing
silhouetted pine trees
fire, candle
booze

One lone driver plying in the distance
crickets, embers
still

Hear that truck hauling for miles
miles and miles
one lone soul
lid-heavy, sated
mellow
alive

Transformation

Found a scrap of scribbling yesterday
looking for a quote from my boss
who died Monday
nice if it had been brilliant like a message he
might conjure
but at least it was there
tiny evidence of a creative pulse

Thoughts of death stroke life
went looking for a sheet of paper
or a notebook
what kind of writer has nothing to write on
aged relies on memory
trying to force feed recovery

Picked up a basketball
hoops
no trace of touch left
finally in, stuck in the bottom of the net
couldn't jump high enough to touch it
what was that, four inches?

I do not recognize that guy in the mirror
guy in the window
where did all that come from
what happened to my youth
fitness, slim countenance
where did me go amigo?

My eyes glaze over

Karlsruhe

Images capture glimpses
innocent times
places faces
spaced out heads
palace and chalice, strangers
no malice intended

Spies lurk everywhere
everyone's a suspect
but tokes and jokes
smoke in bubbles
burst on the lawn
tear down walls of fear

Sometimes you can tell
bell beads candle
long hair unkempt
bleary-eyed grins can be nice
to rely on
yet even narcs can be heads

Wasted tired drawn
but feeding the head
helps the body along
though not strong
all the love energy needed, more
saved in the storeroom of the heart

Sitting neath a palace wall
scrawl black on white

fill lines empty times
photos and rhyme
who knows what if anything
will turn up

Pause laugh
screeching loons preach loony tunes
revere revelry of long ago
has the finest hour passed
did idealism die
the dream commit suicide

For Lisa Marie

In a sentiment I started a long time ago
I tried to tell you
just how much I need you

You were my garden, I said
my fountain of youth
you were proof
God made sunny days and sandy beaches
for lovers

I also tried to tell you I'd be honest
as I could be
and still be me

So you see
when I spend time by myself
get a little lost in myself
commune with nature
sometimes I get lost

But always find my way home

Home to the garden
the fire that warms me
home to the love that feeds me
back to the place I most want to be

Back together
always together
you and me

Hiroshima

Screaming faces lined with pain
death rained from the sky
snatched the breath
took the life of the city

Years later children play
monuments stand, a burned-out hulk remains
the pain is gone
don't let the memory fade

Meander

Charting paths, uncharted wrath
        blazing conifer
        fire from above
Heat and light, stillness might
        soaken clumps of newsprint lump
        fill the palace of love

Failure fits in a sitzbath
        scar-faced landlords loosen ties
        hiding the sky at night
Fat haughty robins wolf turning
        worms down
        burning again

Sevender lavender singular fill
        a fiend to woo thirst
        slaked-first hate
Crawls up from the gurgling goo

Languid

Between two succulent lips
my tongue passes
flicks
licks
captures the essence of you

From the bottom of your soul
your essence drips
elixir of Venus
intoxicating
bringing this rider home

The wondrous sweet of your body stays
long after you are gone
all that I am become falls aside
when I lose myself
in the cozy warmth of your charms

No place finer could I find to die
clutched to your breast
pulled tight
caressed
by your loving silky arms

Come to me tonight my love
I will come with you
pleasure spectacular
feast, bounty
all in the essence of you

Trade Mission in Kobe

Denisov and Kistanov
Russian soldiers on the diplomatic front
took a look at the front and rear of my wife
their minds wandered from vodka and
propaganda
to brandy
songs and sex

But what can you expect

What better way to improve relations
than have relations
with a foreigner
in a foreign land

Gotta hand it to 'em
they've got good taste

Mexico Melancholy

The trees are filled with diamonds
as I cuddle with my golden eyes
the pattern of sun rain sun
begins anew

One ear hears the drops from above
the other nestled in cozy flesh
picks up stomach sounds
your heartbeat
the flow of life

From the still pools of your eyes
the first hint of sorrow comes
a glisten
a dew drop
then a deep-breasted shudder as you begin to
cry

Political Cartoons

They might be giants
they might be bugs
this might
be
the Bugs Bunny Hour

Idiots
can scare
hell out of you
when they're in
positions of power

One Day

A long time ago
in our paradise
on the coast of Mexico
I understood why
accepted the fact
someday you would go

Sierra Madre warm wind
margaritas on the patio
jazz
cigarettes
we toasted the sea
treasured life
loved each other
gave thanks to God
for you and me as we

Now I cast my eyes
to the sea
hoping for a glimpse of you
coming over the horizon
knowing somewhere
you're lost in time
out of sight
in another land
but never out of my mind

Times have changed
people come
and go
yet Vallarta remains like yesterday

I'm still waking with the sun
or staying up til dawn
knowing you're somewhere on the road
hoping you long
for you and me as we

Tonight I'll search a darkening sky
look for a sign
in lightning and thunder
wonder how to get through to you
make my luck run true
and once again cast my eyes on you

Choice

Dangerous days
fractured families
hardened hearts
at His feet is where the healing starts

Father God blessed Savior
light of the universe
humble me Lord
so I walk your way not mine
help me release desire for control
experience life divine

It isn't about who is strongest
biggest or loudest
not who has the most toys
when they die

More than a sales pitch
more than a bumper sticker
more than misguided
that's a dangerous lie

Some sell a dream
as reality
while they sell their souls
to give the devil his due

No matter how they ply you
with sweet talk and promises
don't give in
don't let it happen to you

People will tell you
it's not a big deal
you've' really got nothing to lose
yet in the end
heaven or hell
depend on the path you choose

Nowhere

It's been so long
since I've been to the valley
so long you said when
you walked out the door

I never believed it
would happen to me
never believed
I could fall so far
miss the daylight
the sunshine
the smile in your eyes
so long

But the wake up call says
there's no one there
there's no time to look back
with sorrow

There's no choice
but to believe in the choice
believe that the voice
screaming inside
"Wrong, you idiot"
is wrong

Frolic

Mundanity
mendaciousness
goodness gracious me
Mother Nature's symphony
can be so simple grand wonderful
cruel

Fire-breathing mountain
river of rocks and mud
jagged light
starry night
sweet grass tall trees
the sea

Met the delusions of grandeur
today
they swept as a horde
over the hill
and screamed
"No prisoners"

Wave after wave came
I was carried away
to where I can't say
cajoled
fondled
screwed

Everything

Embarrassed to show my face around
the streets of our old hometown
dreams so high when we went away
how quickly they went awry

Now I'm back here by myself
tail dragging low
my lady's long gone
everything went wrong

Seemed so promising at the time
this new world of ours
it was there at our fingertips
but suddenly slipped away

Now I'm left here by myself
energy fading fast
my lady's gone
everything went wrong

Will we ever recapture the feeling
when love was new
the world was ours
every day was better than the last

Or are we destined
to search every corner
looking for love
trying to forget the past

Still won't show my face around
in this or any town
not without you by my side
and loving me again

Shame you're out there by yourself
while I'm here alone
when I was holding you tight
everything was right

So catch a plane
find your way back
if the feeling's still in your heart
say you love me again

We shouldn't be by ourselves
not one minute more
when I'm holding you tight
everything will be all right

Babe

It's easy, she said
with her eyes, golden
her lips, soft
her thighs
her smile
just open up, she said
and I did
and my God
it was
easy

End

Seems like weeks
spent every night
tossing and turning no sleep
I've been waiting for your call
but then it comes
and there's no love on the end of the line

It's clear sweetheart
no warmth in your voice
ice surges over the airwaves
I know before
I put down the phone
that baby it's the end of the line

What happened to this perfect love
that started out so warm and wild
and who's the man that's loving you
the way I used to all through the night

I thought we had a love for keeps
it seemed we would last forever
but now there's another man holding you close
the way I used to all through the night

I've spent every day
hours on end
can't stop thinking of you
still holding onto hope
you'll come back by
but know it's likely the end of the line

Crazy I know
waiting for you
hoping everything will be all right
there's too much heartache
to throw what we had away
and say it's the end of the line

What happened to this perfect love
it started out so warm and wild
and who's the man that's loving you
the way I used to all through the night

I thought we had a love for keeps
it seemed we would last forever
but now there's another man holding you close
the way I used to all through the night

So if it's true I can't count on you
to be my lover my friend my life
I'll pack my bags
catch the next train
knowing I'll be loving you
to the end of the line

Until the end of time

Holding On

It's but a single grain from the sands of time
        but it's mine, it's mine and I'll live it
I'll not let the ghost of opportunity lost
        haunt me day and night

I don't want to be a writer who doesn't write anymore
        or a poet who creates no more rhyme
Perhaps an ego thing but if I can't be king
        at least a prince, not a pawn

All the words thought but never written
        stories left hanging in the air
Songs never sung, bells never rung
        don't buy that crap anymore

I haven't been far but I'll try for the stars
        gather my strength from the sun
Feel the force, try to find the right course
        and thank God for my chance to run

Whitney

Child of wonder unleashed
born of passion unfurled
haughty, happy
with a doting daddy
who loves you more than you know

Someday my world will be empty
when I'm not here to hold you
not close enough to feed my soul
with your unrelenting love

But no matter how far I stray
no matter how long I'm away
I'll weep openly and often
as I realize how much you're a part of me still
and how much I miss you

Adios

You can go now

I have your pictures in front of me
and spend the days and nights missing you
I see your beautiful eyes that sexy smile
I remember your touch
your hands, your feet, your thighs
and the feel of you and I as we held each other tight
to fend off the storms that raged all around us

Yes, you can go now

It wasn't that long ago when we fought
and you came back to me
hurt that I was trying to scour you
out of my life

There were no pictures up then
nothing to remind me of how much I needed you
how much we've shared, where we've been together
how long and hard I would beg you to come back
if I only thought you would
It was my only defense

Yes, I believe you'll go now

You've succeeded just as you wanted to
making me wholly dependent on your sweet love
I'll stay here with these memories
an ache that won't go away
trying to erase the feeling that I should have done something more
        or something less
that I shouldn't have given in

Now, there is no defense
Just this overwhelming loneliness

Wait

So this is another
wait-until-tomorrow night
what else to do but
get loaded
toasted
my weenie's roasted
your bun is buttered
I offer some mustard
and you say
"Get out of here
don't point that thing at me
it's loaded"

Yesterdaze

Schlock, schlock
the clock strikes on
one two
trip over shoes
hear laughter
echo down a hallway of despair

Glance from the corners of the eyes
no surprise
reeling throbbing
make up a dream
plan scheme
come to the surface for air

Foolish, tawdry
turned into a pumpkin
country bumpkin again
bump on a log
fool on the hill
thanks to you always Paul

Sit staunchly upright
feign smugness
hide fear
ebullient, haughty
timid, crying
life in a fantasy world

Pouring emotions into otherworld visions
tactile pleasures
slumping

shrugging
moving along
is this any way to be

Tossed

Friendship warmth
humanity
yet stuck here on inanity
success many never dreamed of
thrown away

Stand straight on your feet
before you're six feet under
seeing it all
as a great fall
presupposes greatness to begin with

Thank heaven
for the hiding night
away from prying eyes
no need for stories
alibis
glossed over vagaries
falling apart by degrees

Mentally drained
straining to make sense
of insanity
squandered wasted
erased so much time
yet every now and then
a seed

Triumph
terror
rage against the commonplace

today is another chance
tomorrow a mystery

Dreams

Dreams are fantasies
while simple reality
finds few ever at peace
or satisfied

Foot to the floorboard
throttle open wide
maniacal drive

Face paint and camouflage greens
hide the obscene truth
we are all that we seem

So much to be done
some to be undone
so little time

Strangers in the bushes
foes in the trees
faces all around us

Friends compatriots
lend us your eyes
offer your vision again

Capture the barker's spiel
that says come now
come now everyone in

Bring it all together
what happened to Lincoln logs

where is John Logan now

Should be a redcap howling banshee
because she is with me
likes to please me
but sometimes I just need room to breathe

'T Ain't So Joe

Most everyone embellishes most freely admit
some a lot others a little bit

Some untruths are characterized as little white
lies
to protect or soothe or shield innocent eyes
others are designed for devious ends
naked attempts at dominance

Effects on the perpetrator can be narrow or
wide
conscience will dictate how much it eats up
inside

Scariest is a liar caught yet unrepentant of the
lie
while wielding power over who lives and who
dies
crazy to find ourselves in this challenging time
with a leader fully embedded in the Cult of the
Lie

———

You claimed new election laws were Jim Crow
two-point-oh
record turnout shows that isn't so
guess voters didn't get the memo
none were more restrictive than in your own
Delaware
or reliably Democrat New York

Yet it's nothing new no aberration
just another patchwork fable
thrown onto the table
part of a long-standing pattern
of dissimulation

"I'm serious man
my wife was killed by a guy who drunk his
lunch and tee-boned her"
no, the police report said
regrettably
she crossed the centerline into the other driver

First person in your family to attend college
one of many fibs that flushed you out of the
'08 race
but temporary disgrace
hasn't stemmed the tide for a second
nor prevented your and the lies' resurrection

You never attended historically black Delaware
State
full academic scholarship for law school, wrong
in the top half of your class, sorry
you remind us of an ill-intended Mr. Magoo
or Alfred "what me worry?"

Outstanding student in the poli sci department
graduated with three degrees, geez
even you must see
with available records a credible jury
wouldn't hesitate to convict you of perjury

So vaccines weren't available when you took office
never mind the two shots you'd already received
"I didn't condemn the travel shutdown," right
"xenophobic fear-mongering" was your phrase
and now you have your own travel restriction

"I'll shut down the virus not the country" epic fail
"If the prior president had done his job
all people dead would still be alive" not true
the million dead since you came in
tell us, are they all on you?

"Never opposed fracking" though CNN confirmed you did
nor did you get arrested trying to see Mandela, fella
didn't march or get arrested during the Civil Rights movement
not shot at while visiting Iraq
so much blarney must be difficult to keep track

Obfuscating always on illegal immigration
no the border's not in the least bit "closed"
every month sets a new record for illegal entry
while in cover of darkness your charters fly illicit migrants
to unsuspecting communities around the country

Border agents didn't strike people with whips,
get a grip
the number of crossers grows ever higher
yet you have not lifted a finger
and fentanyl streams in
killing a hundred thousand or more every year

"Had a house burn down with my wife in it," no
it was only a small kitchen fire
didn't drive a semi, never appointed to the
Naval Academy
never a full professor at University of
Pennsylvania
"raised in the Puerto Rican community," all
hooey

Never written Law Review articles on the right
to privacy
flunking a law school class for plagiarism didn't
stop your stealing
Golda Meir never asked you to be her Egypt
liaison
Tree of Life synagogue folks said you didn't
speak there
that supposed Amtrak conductor chat would
have been 15 years after he retired

Claimed DC rioters killed a cop — no, Corn Pop
"no one lost health insurance due to
Obamacare," untrue
jobs economy inflation all grist for repeated
fabrication
Build Back Better cost nothing, no debt

lies keep mounting and we're not even to
Hunter or Afghanistan yet

"Never spoke to my son about his overseas
business dealings"
laptop was "Russia disinformation"
these layers of deceit and untruth so deep
c'mon, Big Guy, showing the lie to your denial
records show you met with at least 14 of the
players

Bragged about threatening to withhold a billion
unless Ukraine fired the prosecutor looking at
Burisma corruption
and that voice mail you left Hunter
saying he was probably in the clear
is that just a figment of our imagination?

A "commander in chief" apparently unaware
of the meaning of the phrase "stolen valor"
claims his son died in Iraq offers lies about
purple hearts
"God's truth, my word as a Biden"
tells us exactly what that is worth

Afghanistan you called "an extraordinary
success"
tell that to the families of the 13 dead soldiers:
Hoover Pichardo Gee Lopez
Page Sanchez Espinoza Schmitz
McCollum Merola Nikoui Soviak Knauss

Billions in weapons and infrastructure left behind
we'll never know for sure how many Americans and allies
you said al-Qaeda was gone, wrong
and the under-oath testimony of your generals
to Senate Armed Services
showed you lied about their advice

———

Sad to realize only a small number of these lies
are designed to shield the family criminal enterprise

So much of it is just who you are
and this massive inflation of untruth, not transitory
tells all the world that the supposed "Free World leader"
is bumbling, dangerous and our most consequential prevaricator

Keep

Streetlights glow
freeform seep
you're the reason
I keep coming back
one last stab at fantasy
toss the mice
see how their eyes roll
snake eyes
sevens
boxcars to hide in
feel the clickety clack
will it ever come back
steer onto the right track
that leads
and leads
and leads on

Loaded again
confidence eroded again
that same old feeling
in the pit of the stomach
don't know if I can stomach it anymore

How Long

She says I have a sickness breath
which sets me wondering
healthy as I feel
if it’s the stench of death

Few know when the time will come
what hour of the day
day of the week
the heart will say it's done

Baker looms
trees stop the breeze

Sitting in the fleeting sun
thoughts flood
shadows lengthen
pray our love has just begun

Angel

Angel of mercy came in the daytime
burst on the scene like a beauty queen
knocked the sox off me

Yes you cried when the clouds rolled in
sure you sobbed when the screen went dark
but sunlight and smiles will be your legacy
your warmth and sweetness will haunt my
memory
if ever you go away

As the shadows dance by the fire's glow
I'm loving this romance
glad we took the chance to care

A penny for your thoughts
a fortune in your smile
as the evening fades
worries pass away
soothed by the way you make this house a
home

Away

Call to the wind
cry out loud
this ain't no holy land
but it's part of the plan
a place away
stay away get away home

Banshee scream in the middle of the night
starlight
screech owl peers through the trees
what does it take to please you
where are you tonight
why

Eagle's beak bloody
Prometheus' red
flood's coming
trouble 'round the bend
find truth
pursue beauty
to hell with significance
dream
this trance will lead anywhere
but here

Rules Are Meant To Be Broken

Son it ain’t hard to sonnet
it's just how you look upon it
pick something timeless rhyming not rhymeless
give it a rhythm and begin it

Show what a mess it's in
we’re in
is anybody in
you can't help but win

Fourteen lines to be relevant, funny
poignant, new
different
perhaps agin' the government

so what if a lifetime of searching for the right rhyme
is no more than crumpled paper in the ashcan of time

Ending

So you think you're so damn experienced
you think you've seen it all
you happened to be there when Kennedy fell
you happened to be there when the wall came
down
but baby you ain't seen nothin' yet

Destruction is a glacier, it comes day by day
it's cyclical, annual, marching ever on
no fundamentalist jargon can stop the tide
the bottom line may get top dollar every time
but baby you ain't seen nothin' yet

High jinks and high times are bringing on high
noon
every form of lowlife crawling from the gutter
utter confusion is about to reign
yellow and acid, white hot and fiery
baby you ain't seen nothin' yet

Floods in the south, quakes in the west
twisters to the gut of our country
the time of Watts and the time of Watt
ain't got nothin' on the riot ahead
you ain't seen nothin' yet

Repeat

Heavens wide open
rain pouring down
one more for the road and I'll go
women look the same
strange and unattainable
time this town got a look at my heels
so I can really start to feel again

Play the fool
scare 'em away
who knows why
whenever hope shows it's scrambled away
egg on the face
omlet Hamlet dammit why
heavens cry
this stormy weather is the perfect backdrop
to head for the blacktop and fly

Self-centered hyperbole
dreams that never will be
what an ugly legacy
who cares anyway anyway
one more chance
to throw stones at the mirror
see it smash
and know that in a flash
it'll be good as new

Love of My Life

You're a symphony of colors
a golden field
a rainbow day
the sun coming through at last

Birds in flight
can't touch the thrill
of what I'm feeling
for you still

I refuse to believe you won’t still love me
the way you loved me before
Never accept I won’t ever see you
by the light of dawn anymore

Remember sweet times holding each other
close
so much in love
so much time ahead
so little if only we knew

So tonight I scream to God above
to solve the riddle, show the way
to release your love, let it free
see if it comes ebbing back to me

I'd give anything to see you spread your wings
and still want to stay with me
I want to be your strength, shoulder to cry on
your counterpoint and harmony

I'd fill every hollow in your heart
pull every star from the sky
to make a crown
for my golden eyes

My wishes were fulfilled, my heart was captured
the day you came into my life
everything I've ever wanted walked down the aisle with you
the day you became my wife

You Again

Still the cutest thing in the world
snug as a button
savvy as a cat
sweet kiss hot as the sun

A wild time a crazy night
bliss and spite
wily and frightful
a mix of black and blues
good news and bad
the most wonderful woman
I ever had

So fear not dread not
sweet little lady
tight as dreadlocks
free as the rivers run

Through sorrow ecstasy
fun fear fantasy
I promise endlessly
to love irresistible irrepressible
sinful yet respectable
effervescent incandescent
happy sassy classy
wonderful you

Moments

These few moments are all we have
let’s treasure them as we hold each other
make them last until morning comes
and we go our separate ways

Good times between us pass so quickly
we need to realize how lucky we are
to share this uncommon intensity
for tomorrow it may all be gone

There's sadness underpinning this heartfelt love
so deep and strong shining so clear
it's that the good times don't last forever
and seem too easily quickly forgotten

Simple pleasures quiet times
a smile, a song so romantic
these are the things we need to remember
because we don't know how soon they'll be gone

So these few moments that we have together
let's treasure them and hold each other
make them last til morning comes or days beyond
til we go our separate ways

Because these few moments will pass so fast
please realize how lucky we are
to share this uncommon intensity

for tomorrow it may all be gone

Outta Here

There's refuge in a starry night
an escape hatch to another stratosphere
no need for rhyme or reason
no seasonally adjusted forecasts to consider

And consider this
it's a damn sight better than biding your time
or kissing your ass goodbye

So let me out
turn out the lights
last one through lock the door

Boring as it may be to most of you
empty as it may be to the rest
I'm booking passage on a midnight express
no more, no less

Let's fire up the engines
turn on the afterburners
and jet away from here

I want to be missing when the missile hits
I want to be gone when the lights go down
there won't be any curtain calls this time
no ovations, no survivors

No One

Looking into your golden eyes
I catch a glimpse of paradise
dreams and visions
two hearts as one
a love burning brighter than the brightest sun

Watching you breathing soft in sleep
a treasure I want to keep
I feel honesty, passion
two souls entwined
fire to light up the darkest night

For there's no other woman like you babe
no one could do to me the things that you do
it's magic, fantastic, amazing but true
that there's no one in this world
no one in any world
who could take the place of you

Tough times in the past have hurt you
we don't always treat each other right
but look in my eyes babe
deep into your soul
you'll find a love that will continue to grow

Whatever you do let's stick this through
give our love another chance to shine
look into your heart
and this heart of mine
you'll find a bond to stand the test of time

Because there's no other woman like you babe
no one could do to me the things that you do
it's magic, fantastic, amazing but true
that there's no one in this world
no one in any world
who could take the place of you

And there's no other man like me babe
no one could love you as deep as I do
it's magic, fantastic, amazing but true
that there's no one in this world
no one in any world
who could take the place of you

Musclehead

Sax and violins
brass and woodwinds
a duo, a trio
a quarter to five
a combination plate
too late the question
the equation
the equator
the meaning of life

Sex and violence
triple sec and treble damages
rampage through the jungle
bungle a chance
that fateful glance
a smirk
a smile
in and out
the onrushing tide

Lisa

Coloriscura lady
purple and lavender
what shades move you
what passions
lurk
do you get red
with anger or green
is there envy in your eyes
are you all that you seem
is this a daydream
in black and white
or a panorama
in living
lovecolor

Donnybrook

Wizard, wizard
where is your magic
what tragic scenes have you set today
where does the time fly
how high the sky
and why so sad on this sunny day

Though Jack was nimble
they cut him to the quick
impaled him on a candlestick
reamed him, gored him
tossed him out with the trash
and said, "Take that
you son of a bitch
let's see how far you can walk
with a monkey on your back”

Blue Collar Blues

Somebody said the good life is dead
today I'm bound to agree
got bounced out the door
another out of work deplorable
screwing up the recovery
cuz I'm lazy

News called my kind an economic indicator
lagging behind people in the mainstream
got my beer and my bread
getting fat in front of the teevee
this recession's no obsession with me
cuz I'm lazy

Ten and a Wakeup

Watching waiting
anticipating
the ring of the phone
the call to go home
I can't be free to just be me
I'm captive prisoner
against my will
so here I sit on the window sill
gazing at nameless faces below
wanting and needing the power to grow
to be free of conscription
out of restriction
into the life
the land that I love

www.ingramcontent.com/pod-product-compliance
Lightning Source LLC
LaVergne TN
LVHW090133160826
845673LV00017B/2461

9798373421126